Yoga
For Energy
Monique Joiner Siedlak

OSHUN
PUBLICATIONS

Printed in the United States of America

Second Edition 2017

ISBN-13: 978-1-948834-60-5

Publisher
www.oshunpublications.com

Disclaimer
All the material contained in this book is provided for educational and informational purposes only. No responsibility can be taken for any results or outcomes resulting from the use of this material. While every attempt has been made to provide information that is both accurate and effective, the author does not assume any responsibility for the accuracy or use/misuse of this information.

Notice

This book is not intended as a substitute for the medical advice of physicians. The reader should regularly consult a physician or therapist in matters relating to his/her health and particularly with respect to any symptoms that may require diagnosis or medical attention.

Yoga Poses Photos

Pixabay.com

Freepik.com

Dreamstime.com

Cover Design by Monique Joiner Siedlak

Cover Image by Pixabay.com

Logo Design by Monique Joiner Siedlak

Logo Image by Pixabay.com

Sign up to email list: www.mojosiedlak.com

Other Books in the Series

Yoga for Beginners

Yoga for Stress

Yoga for Back Pain

Yoga for Weight Loss

Yoga for Flexibility

Yoga for Advanced Beginners

Yoga for Fitness

Yoga for Runners

Yoga for Your Sex Life

Yoga: To Beat Depression and Anxiety

Yoga for Menstruation

Table of Contents

Introduction to This Book

When you're stuck in an afternoon rut or waking up bleary-eyed after a late night, yoga may not be the first factor you move to for a jolt of energy.

Turns out, besides improving sleep quality, alleviating stress and anxiety and boosting overall physical wellness, yoga can furthermore be a great natural energy-booster.

Yoga works on unblocking stuck pieces of energy along the spine. You create what the yogis describe as prana, or life force, into the back and all these regions of the body through breathing and action. You're moving the circulatory system and waking the nervous system to bring fresh life into the body.

As we remain seated throughout the day, the energy in the spine becomes caught and stagnant. So when we lengthen the spine, it stimulates and energizes the nervous system. That's why the backbends are so exhilarating. And when you're moving in a back-bending manner, you're also bringing more attention to the heart and opening the chest muscles, which clears the body.

These poses engage your leg and buttocks muscles, which are your biggest muscles. This signifies that your heart will work harder to push extra blood to this area. This increased heart rate will also expand your breathing rate.

Bridge Pose (Setu Bandha Sarvangasana)

The Bridge Pose is a beginning backbend that helps to open your chest and stretch your thighs.

How to Do

To begin, lie supine (on your back). Fold your knees and keep your feet hip distance apart on the floor, ten to twelve inches from your pelvis, with your knees and ankles in a straight line. With your arms beside your body, place your palms faced down.

Breathe in, while slowly lifting your lower back, middle back and upper back off the floor. Gently roll in your shoulders. Touch your chest to your chin without bringing the chin down. Support your weight with your shoulders, arms, and feet. Feel your buttocks firm up in this pose. Both your thighs should be parallel to each other and to the floor.

You could interlock your fingers and push your hands on the floor to lift your torso a bit more up if you want or you could support your back with your palms. Keep breathing easily.

Hold this pose for a minute or two and then exhale as you gently release the pose.

Benefits

The Bridge Pose strengthens your back, opens the chest, and improves your spinal mobility.

Tips

After you roll your shoulders under, be sure not to pull them away from your ears. This often overstrains your neck. Raise the tops of your shoulders toward your ears and push your inner shoulder blades away from your spine.

King Dancer Pose (Natarajasana)

The King Dancer Pose is an intermediate, standing yoga pose which merges the demanding aspects of balancing with a backbend. There are two alternatives which are frequently practiced. The first one requires grasping the lifted leg with one hand, while the second is an advanced pose that requires grasping the raised foot with both hands overhead.

How to Do

Start in the Mountain Pose. Move your weight on to your left foot and bend your right knee to bring your foot towards your right buttock. Grasp the inside of your right foot with your right hand and bring your left hand up to your hip.

Locate your balance. Lengthen your tailbone downwards and tone your abdomen. Start to push your right foot into your right hand to ease your back foot rising up behind and away from you. Keep your right knee hugging in towards your middle and not out to the side. While your foot rises up, slant your torso forward, providing a lift through your chest.

To offset the compression in your lower back, maintain an engaged core. Bring the bend out of your lower back, and into your upper back. Lift your left hand up to the ceiling, with your thumb aiming backwards and your pinky finger aiming forwards. Shift your gaze up and breathe. Remain in the pose for twenty to thirty seconds, and slowly release. Repeat on the alternative side, maintaining for the same period of time.

Benefits

The King Dancer pose releases tension in the angle and foot, helping to prevent injury and develops a sense of balance and focus. It also stretches your thighs and shoulders while it strengthens your spine and legs

Tips

Most beginners tend to cramp in the back of their thighs when lifting the leg. Make sure to keep the ankle of your raised foot flexed.

Half Lord of Fishes Pose (Ardha Matsyendrasana)

The Half Lord of Fishes Pose is a moderate to intense twist that encourages length of your spine, a base stretch for your outer hips, and brings forth growth through the chest and shoulders.

How to Do

Begin in a seated position with your legs straight in front of you. Bring in your knees up and bend them with the purpose of your feet are now flat on the floor. This is your beginning position. Bring your right leg beneath your left leg. Maintain your left leg in the starting position. Your right leg should bend at the knee and then keep close to your hip.

Taking your left leg, cross it over the left knee. Set your left foot flat on the floor on the outside of your right knee. Bring your right arm and reach up. Next slowly bend your arm at the elbow and place your elbow on your left knee. Take your left arm and place behind your back and use for a base.

Breathe in and out while either turning your head opposite to the way your back is stretching, or you can turn your head with your back.

Benefits

The Half Lord of Fishes Pose can restore and improve spinal range of motion. It also beneficial for backaches.

Tips

Maintain your right leg extended if you cannot steadily tuck it beneath your left buttock. Squeeze the left knee with your right arm if that feels better than bringing the right elbow outside the left knee. If you normally use a blanket or other prop under your sit bones for seated poses, it's fine to do that here as well.

One Legged King Pigeon Pose (Eka Pada Rajakapotasana)

The One-Legged King Pigeon Pose typically known as the Pigeon Pose is a strong hip-opener that can help increase your flexibility and the scope of motion in your hip joints.

How to Do

Start off in Downward-Facing Dog pose, or on your hands and knees in the Table Pose. Bringing your left knee in the middle of your hands, place your left ankle close your right wrist. Lengthen your right leg behind you so that your kneecap and the top of your foot and toes lie on the floor.

Pushing with your fingertips, raise your upper body away from your thigh. Elongate the front of your body, while releasing your tailbone back toward your heels. Work on aligning your hips and the front side of your torso to the front of your mat.

Drawing down through your front-leg shin, balance out your weight equally in the middle of your right and left hips.

Flexing the front of your foot, press down through the tops of all five of your toes and the back of your foot, as you set your focus towards the floor.

Hold this pose for up to one minute. To release the pose, gather your back toes, raise your back knee off the mat, and then push yourself back into the Downward-Facing Dog. Repeat this pose for the equal amount of time on the other side.

Benefits

The One-Legged King Pigeon Pose stretches the thighs, groins, and abdomen. It can regularly be felt intensely in particular upper-leg and hip muscles. It eases tension in your chest and shoulders, as it additionally promotes the abdominal organs, which benefits your digestion management.

Tips

For added support, you may place a thickly folded towel or blanket beneath your hip.

Cobra Pose (Bhujangasana)

The Cobra Pose is a familiar Yoga backbend. When you perform the Cobra Pose, you stretch the front of your torso and spine.

How to Do

Lie face down on the floor. Extend your legs back, with the tops of your feet on the floor. Stretch your hands on the floor beneath your shoulders. Squeeze the elbows back into your body. Push the tops of your feet, thighs, and pubis powerfully into the floor.

On an inhalation, start to straighten your arms to raise your chest off the floor. Go only to a height at which you can sustain a connection throughout your pubis to your legs. Press your tailbone toward the pubis and raise the pubis toward your navel. Narrow the hip, compressing but don't harden your buttocks.

Firm the shoulder blades against the back, puffing the side ribs forward. Lift through the top of the sternum but avoid pushing the front ribs forward, which only hardens the lower back. Distribute the backbend evenly throughout the full spine.

Hold the pose anywhere from fifteen to thirty seconds, breathing freely. Release back to the floor with an exhalation.

Benefits

The Cobra Pose is best known for its capability to build up the flexibility of your spine. It stretches the chest along with strengthening your spine and shoulders. It further assists in opening the lungs and stimulating the abdominal organs, improving digestion.

An energizing backbend, the Cobra Pose can reduce stress and fatigue. It also firms and tones the shoulders, abdomen, and buttocks, and assists in easing back pain.

Tips

The Cobra Pose will be able to energize and warm up the body, getting it ready for the deeper backbends in your yoga routine.

Sphinx Pose (Ardha Bhujangasana)

The Sphinx Pose is an adjusted form of the Cobra Pose to aid beginners makes their way easier into it. This pose is furthermore good for people who have lower backache as it has fewer arches and therefore reduces the compression on the spine.

How to Do

Start with lying on your stomach, legs stretched out and steadily together, lengthening the legs by extending the big toe and inner muscles of the foot. Turn your thighs inwardly to the ground to help in widening your back.

Attempt to lengthen your legs and toes past the loosened length. The stretch of your coccyx or tailbone should be progressively increasing. Confirm that your hips are fixed, but not actually hard. Allow your focus to be calm. Allow your forearms be paralleled to the floor beneath you. As you inhale, raise your upper torso from the floor to form a slight backbend.

Focusing on your lower belly, lightly raise it above the floor so that a rounded shape is made. Stay in this pose for about 6-10 breaths. End by exhaling as you relax your stomach and upper torso back to the floor. By turning your head to one side, complete this pose. Leave go of all the tension in the last exhalation. If you want to, you may repeat the pose, and end by turning your head to the opposite side.

Benefits

The Sphinx Pose stretches chest and lungs, shoulders, and abdomen as well as strengthens the spine. It firms the buttocks and stimulates abdominal organs. Improves your blood circulation in the hip joints while relieving back pain. Best of all, the Sphinx Pose helps to relieve stress.

Tips

To help support the lifting of your belly, roll up a towel or blanket and arrange it in a U-shape on the floor, under the pubic bone or use a bolster instead. If your head feels too heavy to hold, you can support it with your hands.

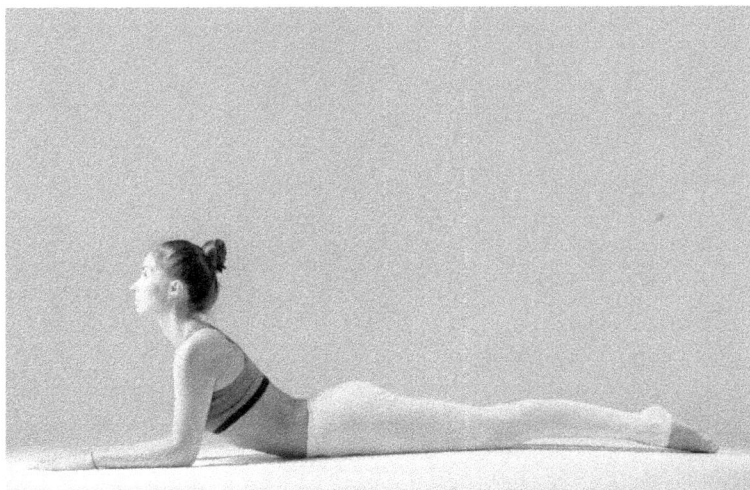

Upward Bow Pose (Urdhva Dhanurasana)

The Upward Bow Pose is considered an advanced yoga pose that stretches and opens your entire body. The Upward Bow Pose can be a difficult pose to attain with the correct alignment.

How to Do

Begin in Corpse Pose. Bending your knees draw your heels toward your hips, positioning them as close as possible to your sitting bones. The bottom of your feet should be hip-width apart and pressed against the floor.

Make ready your body for the pose by raising your hips high off the floor. Drawing your back up into an arch, keep your shoulders steadily planted. Your pose should bear a resemblance to that of the Bridge Pose. Keep this pose for a few breaths, maintaining your pelvis and torso raised and your chin up. Drop your hips back to the floor to get ready for the full bow.

Raise your arms straight up from your sides, starting with the backs of your hands, and bend your elbows as they get nearer to the floor. Place your hands on either side of your head, with your palms down and your fingers pointing toward the shoulders. Your elbows should be pointing up at the ceiling, with your forearms perpendicular to the floor. Keep your elbows pulled inward without crowding around the ears and neck.

Press your feet into the floor and again lift up at the hips as you performed earlier. Hold for a couple of breaths. Push into the hands once more, then breathe in and rise to the top of your head, elevating your shoulders off of the mat. Keep your shoulders squeezed into the back but pulled away from your ears. Maintain this position for a couple of breaths in addition.

At this point, push equally into both your hands and feet, breathe out and raise your head totally off of the ground. Straighten your arms as you lift, maintaining your shoulders and tailbone tightly drawn into the back. Lengthen your legs as your arms straighten out up until you reach the maximum height of your back bend.

Maintain this pose for a few steady breaths, increasing from five to ten-second counts if you're comfortable. To release the pose, lower back down to the top of the head. Put your chin in toward your sternum before lowering your hips and torso to the ground to help you prevent neck injury.

Benefits

The Upward Bow Pose aids in strengthening your legs, the forearms, shoulders, and wrists, helps in toning the buttocks and is an excellent stretch for the biceps and triceps.

This yoga pose is also very helpful in increasing the strength and flexibility of your back, spine, and abdomen.

Tips

Your knees and feet have a tendency to spread as you rise into this pose, which constricts the lower back. In the beginning position, you can loop and secure a strap around your thighs, just above your knees, to hold your thighs at hip width and parallel to each other. To keep your feet from turning out, position a block between them, with the bases of your big toes pressing the ends of the block. You'll find that as you go up, you will press the feet into the block.

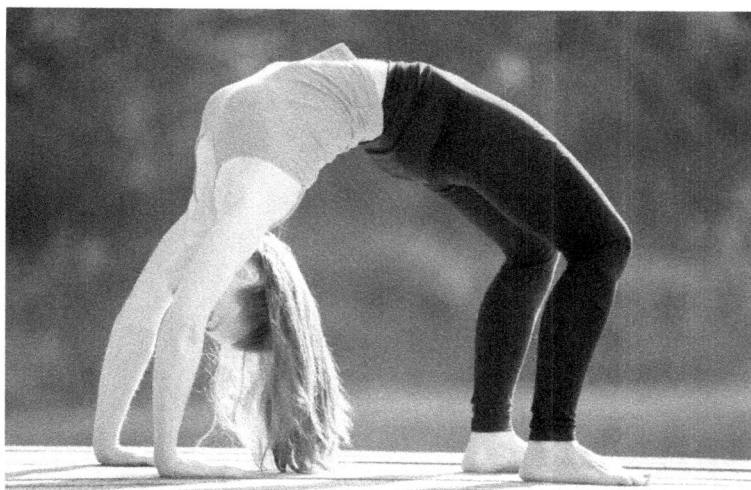

Downward Facing Dog Pose (Adho Mukha Svanasana)

Downward Facing Dog Pose is one of the traditional Sun Salutation sequences poses. It's also an excellent yoga asana all on its own.

How to Do

Begin with your hands and knees in a tabletop position. Make sure your shoulders are aligned above your wrists and your hips are aligned above your knees. Come to a flat back by lengthening the spine. Place your head and neck in a non-aligned position, staring down in the direction of the floor.

Breathe out and raise your knees away from the floor. At the start, keep your knees slightly bent and your heels lifted away from the floor. Lengthen your tailbone positioned from the back of your pelvis and press it slightly toward the pubis. Alongside this tension, raise the resting bones in the direction of the ceiling, and from your inner ankles pull the inner legs up into the groin.

Followed by letting your breath out, push your top thighs back and extend your heels against or down toward the floor. Making sure that you do not lock them, straighten your knees and steady your outer thighs, rolling the upper thighs inward slightly, narrowing the front of the pelvis.

Firming the outer arms, press the bottoms of your index fingers assertively into the floor. From these two points, lift alongside the inside of your arms from the wrists to the tops of the shoulders. Firm your shoulder blades against your back then widen them and draw them toward the tailbone. Keep your head between your upper arms; not allowing it to simply hang.

Continue in this pose somewhere between one to three minutes. Afterward, bend your knees to the floor with a breath and repose in the Child's Pose.

Benefits

Downward Facing Dog pose can help decrease back pain through strengthening the whole back and shoulder girdle. It aids in stronger hands, wrists, the Achilles tendon, low-back, hamstrings, and calves, as well as increasing the full-body circulation. Elongates your shoulders and shoulder blade area. Decrease in tension and headaches by elongating the cervical spine and neck and relaxing the head. It can also lessen anxiety and expand your respiration

Tips

You can alleviate the burden on your wrists by employing a block beneath your palms or you can be capable of completing the pose upon your elbows. By lifting your hands on blocks or the seat of a chair, you can help to release and open your shoulders.

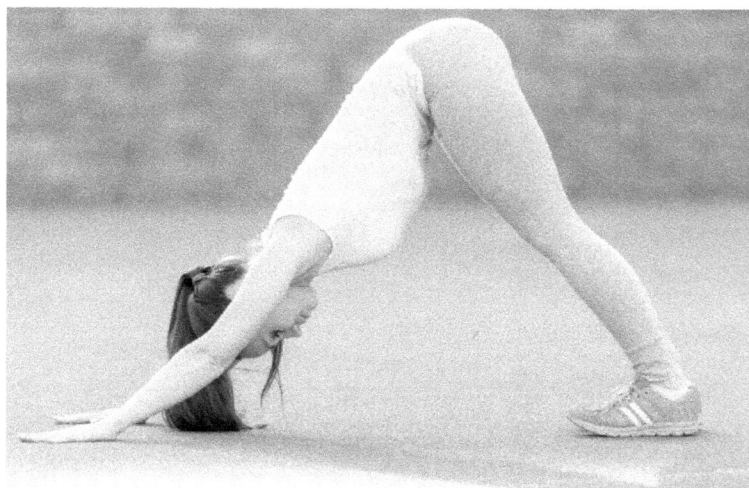

Upward Facing Dog Pose (Urdhva Mukha Svanasana)

Upward Facing Dog Pose is one of the most commonly known, as well as Downward Dog Pose, and recognized yoga pose due to its many benefits and healing uses. Similar to the Cobra Pose, it is thought of as one of the simplest of the back-bending poses and is implemented during the traditional Sun Salutation sequence.

How to Do

Lie face down on the floor. Stretch your legs back, with the tops of your feet on the floor. Bend your elbows and stretch your palms on the floor at the side of your waist so that your forearms are somewhat erect to the floor.

Breathe in and press your inner hands firmly into the floor and somewhat back, similar to trying to push yourself forward along the floor. Then at the same time, straighten your arms and lift your torso up and your legs a few inches off the floor on an intake breath. Keep the thighs firm and somewhat turned inward, the arms firm and turned out so the elbow creases face forward.

Press your tailbone toward your pubis and lift pubis toward your navel. Contract the hip positions. Stiffen but do not totally harden the buttocks.

Steady your shoulder blades against the back and puff the side ribs forward. Lift through the top of the sternum but make an effort not to push the front ribs forward. It will prompt the lower back to tighten. You will at that point look forward or you can angle your head towards the back slightly, remembering to take care not to constrict the back of your neck and the tightening of your throat.

Even though Upward Facing Dog Pose is one position used in the traditional Sun Salutation sequence, you can correspondingly practice this pose independently, maintaining the pose fifteen to thirty seconds, inhaling slowly. Release back to the floor or lift into the Downward Facing Dog pose along with an exhalation.

Benefits

Upward Facing Dog helps open the chest and strengthens the whole body and aligns the spine and invigorates nervous system and the kidneys.

Tips

Performing Upward Facing Dog will elongate and strengthen your whole body. You can use it as a backbend by itself, or as a transition for even deeper backbends.

Plank Pose (Kumbhakasana)

As part of the Sun Salutation sequence, the Plank Pose is an arm balancing yoga pose that aids in tightening up your abdominal muscles and strengthening your arms and spine.

How to Do

This pose very similar to as if you were about to undertake a push-up. After completing the Downward Facing Dog, bring your hips forward till your shoulders are over your wrists and your entire body is in one straight line from the top of your head to your heels.

Be sure that your hips don't drop toward the floor or elevated up in the direction of the ceiling. Spreading out your fingers, push them down and balance on your palms. Bend your elbows and remember not to lock them.

Push back through your heels. Shift your shoulders away from your ears. Keeping your neck aligned with your spine, look towards the floor.

Benefits

The Plank Pose tones all the core muscles of the body, including the abdomen, chest, and low back. It strengthens the arms, wrists, and shoulders, and is often used to prepare the body for more challenging arm balances. Plank also strengthens the muscles surrounding the spine which improves posture.

Tips

When practicing the Plank Pose for several minutes, it will help builds endurance and stamina, while toning the nervous system.

Dolphin Plank Pose (Makara Adho Mukha Svanasana)

The Dolphin Plank Pose is an intermediate level invigorating yoga pose that aids in toning the abdominal muscles.

How to Do

Begin in Downward Facing Dog. Move your weight forward so that your shoulders are over your wrists.

Lower your forearms, One by one, to the floor with your palms facing down. Place your elbows where your hands were, and spread your fingers wide. With your heels over your toes, you want your body to be in one straight line.

Constructing a Yoga Sequence

Here are a few points to keep in mind how to construct a yoga sequence. You are not at a studio, paying to be there. You do not have to exercise for over an hour. Begin with 5-10 minutes. Notice how you feel by the end of this time. If you feel as if you can do more, go ahead. If no, end your routine there.

Start with 5-10 minutes. By the conclusion of that time, notice how you feel. Do you desire to resume? If yes, continue for an extra five minutes and then check in with yourself once more. If not, close your workout.

The same as any physical journey, a yoga sequence has three clear parts.

Your opening or warm-up sequence

You don't want to jump into the main event tight and cold. This is where you move through and loosening up your major muscle groups as well as body parts

Your main sequence

Once you've warmed up, it's time for your main sequence. This component of your sequence is influenced by the goal of your routine. If it's an asymmetrical pose, keep in mind to do both sides and devote about the same time on each side.

The closing or cool down sequence

Now you've completed the principal portion of your yoga practice, it's time to cool down.

About The Author

Monique Joiner Siedlak is a writer, witch, and warrior on a mission to awaken people to their greatest potential through the power of storytelling infused with mysticism, modern paganism, and new age spirituality. At the young age of 12, she began rigorously studying the fascinating philosophy of Wicca. By the time she was 20, she was self-initiated into the craft, and hasn't looked back ever since. To this day, she has authored over 35 books pertaining to the magick and mysteries of life. Her most recent publication is book one of an Urban Paranormal series entitled "Jaeger Chronicles."

Originally from Long Island, New York, Monique is now a proud inhabitant of Northeast Florida; however, she considers herself to be a citizen of Mother Earth. When she doesn't have a book or pen in hand, she loves exploring new places and learning new things. And being the nature lover that she is, she considers herself to be an avid animal advocate.

To find out more about Monique Joiner Siedlak artistically, spiritually, and personally, feel free to visit her **official website**.

Other Books by Monique Joiner Siedlak

Mojo's Wiccan Series

Wiccan Basics

Candle Magick

Wiccan Spells

Love Spells

Abundance Spells

Hoodoo

Herb Magick

Seven African Powers: The Orishas

Moon Magick

Cooking for the Orishas

Creating Your Own Spells

Body Mind and Soul Series

Creative Visualization

Astral Projection for Beginners

Meditation for Beginners

Reiki for Beginners

Thorne Witch Series

The Phoenix

Beautiful You Series

Creating Your Own Body Butter

Creating Your Own Body Scrub

Creating Your Own Body Spray

Mojo's Self-Improvement Series

Manifesting With the Law of Attraction

Stress Management

Jaeger Chronicles

Glen Cove

Connect With Me!

I really appreciate you reading my book! Please leave a review and let me know your thoughts. Here are the social media locations you can find me at:

Like my Facebook Page: www.facebook.com/mojosiedlak

Follow me on Twitter: www.twitter.com/mojosiedlak

Follow me on Instagram: www.instagram.com/mojosiedlak

Follow me on Bookbub: http://bit.ly/2KEMkqt

Sign up to my Email List at www.mojosiedlak.com and receive a free book!

If you enjoyed this book or found it useful I'd be very grateful if you'd post a short review on at your retailer. Your support really does make a difference and I read all the reviews personally so I can get your feedback and make this as well as the next book even better.

www.ingramcontent.com/pod-product-compliance
Lightning Source LLC
Chambersburg PA
CBHW071642040426
42452CB00009B/1738